P9-DTL-565

# ARTIFICIAL INTELLIGENCE

## a revision of
## COMPUTERS THAT THINK?

# ARTIFICIAL INTELLIGENCE

## a revision of
## COMPUTERS THAT THINK?

## MARGARET O. HYDE

ENSLOW PUBLISHERS, INC.

Bloy St. & Ramsey Ave.     P.O. Box 38
Box 777                         Aldershot
Hillside, N.J. 07205     Hants GU12 6BP
U.S.A.                              U.K.

**Library of Congress Cataloging in Publication Data**

Hyde, Margaret Oldroyd, 1917-
    Artificial intelligence.

        Bibliography: p.
        Includes index.
        Summary: Describes artificial intelligence, which is that
branch of computer science devoted to programming computers to
carry out tasks that would require intelligence if they were performed by humans.
        1. Artificial intelligence—Juvenile literature.  2. Computers—
Juvenile literature. [1. Computers. 2. Artificial intelligence] I. Hyde,
Margaret Oldroyd, 1917-    . Computers that think? II. Title.

Q335.H84 1985                    006.3                    85-20573

ISBN 0-89490-124-9

Printed in the United States of America

10 9 8 7 6 5 4 3 2 1

For Emily Goodrich Hyde

# CONTENTS

The author wishes to thank the many people who contributed to this book. Samuel Burstein, Ph.D., Associate Professor of Mathematical Science at New York University, was especially helpful.

# 1.

# MOVING TOWARD THE AGE OF INTELLIGENT MACHINES

Artificial intelligence has so many definitions that it has been compared with the elephant in the story of the blind men who each felt a different part and described the elephant in terms of the part he had felt. However, almost everyone accepts the definition that artificial intelligence is the science of making machines intelligent in order to make them more useful and to understand more about human intelligence.

Is the computer brain of a robot that can recognize a cup an intelligent machine? What about the computers that diagnose diseases and suggest treatment? Or the computer that uses a program designed to beat almost 100 percent of the world's chess players? The answers to these questions depend on your definition of artificial intelligence.

Computers that respond to voice commands and communicate with users in natural language display a kind of artificial intelligence. Consider the system that helps to locate patients who need transplants when an organ suddenly becomes available. For example, a three-year-old boy with brain cancer dies and his parents ask to have his liver used as a transplant for another child. The liver will soon deteriorate, so a search must begin at once. How can a child of similar weight who needs a liver transplant be found quickly? Usually, the answer to this question involves a computer that listens and talks. The conversation follows this pattern:

"I have a liver that is available for transplant," says the human at the hospital where the child died.

"Age of donor?" asks the computer voice at the office of the National Association of Transplant Coordinators in Pittsburgh, Pennsylvania.

"Three years," responds the person.

"What is the donor's weight?" asks the computer.

"Twenty-five pounds," is the response.

"Blood type?"

"B positive," replies the person in the hospital.

"Do you want the entire country searched for need?"

An affirmative response starts the sequence of events that results in the location of a child at a hospital in a nearby state. The person who called the alert line is given a telephone number to call, and the liver transplant operation begins within hours. The computer that both listens and talks is a smart machine that is on call 24 hours a day.

Voice recognition systems are in use in many offices and factories. Your luggage may be sorted at a major airport by the voice commands of baggage handlers. You might edit your videotape by voice commands of "cut" and "splice."

Smart computers are capable of diagnosing diseases with extraordinary accuracy. There are computers that can touch, smell, and see and computers that can recognize spoken commands and answer in everyday English. The EPISTLE program by IBM reads printed material with an optical scanner and does a limited amount of analyzing and editing.

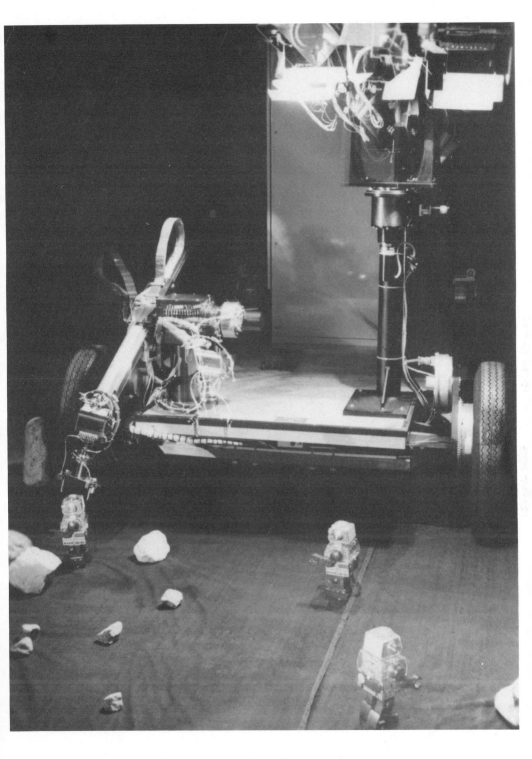

In space, robots with computer brains will take over an increasing number of functions.

—Jet Propulsion Laboratory

Even though great strides are being made with speech recognition systems and with many other kinds of artificial intelligence, computers are still primitive in the areas of abstract reasoning, pattern recognition, and language ability. The storing away of millions of facts does not qualify as thought, but new ways of changing computers from data processors that just receive, store, and display information to artificial brains that can learn, reason, and draw conclusions are causing great excitement in the world of technology and among people who are beginning to use these computers.

Truly intelligent machines are not here yet, nor will they arrive in the very near future. The computers of today, as marvelous and mysterious as they may seem to the average user, are considered very stupid compared with those to come. The computer that can recognize a cup through its TV-camera eye displays some artificial intelligence, but a young child could do the same. An act that seems fairly simple and routine to a person can be an enormously complex process involving hundreds of distinct tasks.

There are probably more nerve cells, or neurons, in the human brain than there are stars in the Milky Way. Educated estimates put the number at one trillion. Now, consider that each of these cells can communicate with as many as 1000 other cells. No wonder many people question whether or not people who reason can make a machine that reasons. Experts are not trying to duplicate all the capabilities of the human brain, but they are finding ways to make computers perform tasks that are far beyond the reach of conventional computers. They talk about computer evolution rather than the computer revolution.

As we move toward more intelligent machines, there is some concern about where smart machines will take us. In a world where knowledge is power and computers command knowledge, will computer achievement play a large part in world power? Japan has announced to the world that it has embarked on a crash program to develop computers that can reason, draw conclusions, make judgments, and understand the written and spoken word. Should the United States be concerned about the Japanese challenge? What is happening in America in the world of artificial intelligence?

Will computers ever be as smart as people? Some computer experts believe that the answer to this question is yes, and that computers  may even surpass people in intelligence. However, they are quick to admit that many things go on in the human mind that we do not understand. Human beings know millions, or even billions, of common-sense things that machines must be taught if they are going to understand the way people do. Something as easy for a child as putting on a sweater is very complicated for a computer. The action must be broken down into detailed steps. If you make a list of every step that is involved,  you will soon see that putting on a sweater is actually a complex process.

As they try to imitate actions that seem easy for a person, artificial intelligence researchers gain new respect for the human brain. The everyday tasks we take for granted are the result of a series of extremely complicated steps that take place in a flash in the human nervous system. For example, unimaginable billions of neurons work simultaneously when you walk down the street and recognize the face of a friend who is walking toward you.

While some scientists feel very positive about teaching computers to become as intelligent as people, others firmly believe that computers can never be programmed to know as much as a person knows and to understand what they know. Certainly, a truly intelligent machine would have to be more than huge numbers of symbols stored in a data base.

Will computers ever be able to exhibit insight, intuition, or inspiration? Will they ever have the ability to understand something suddenly the way humans do? Hubert Dreyfus, a philosopher who has explored computer intelligence for many years, insists that scientists will never be able to formulate a set of rules to describe how people think. No one knows how intelligence works in people, and he believes that the human mind will never be able to explain itself.

Researchers in artificial intelligence reply to Dreyfus by reminding him that at one time it was believed that humans could not fly. Since people do not have wings or feathers like birds, human flight was considered impossible. Who can say whether or not it will ever be possible to build a truly intelligent machine? Certainly, artificial intelligence programs and human thought have much to learn from each other. The possibilities are staggering, and work in the field of artificial intelligence is already beginning to make the world better in exciting ways.

Since a computer can be programmed to do anything that can be expressed in a precise set of instructions, need we fear that artificial intelligence will be used in destructive ways? Herbert A. Simon, a founder of artificial intelligence and Nobel prize winner for his research on decision-making, sees no great reason to fear this kind of knowledge. He suggests that human beings sometimes use power for good and sometimes misuse it. But if one has to choose between knowledge and ignorance, knowledge is better.

Progress in artificial intelligence may enable us to explain human thought by the use of computers and computer programs, and many people will find themselves reconsidering what it means to be human. They may view themselves as colleagues of intelligent machines that augment their own reasoning capacities. Computers that think may also expand the capacity of people to see, hear, feel, and smell, providing wonderful experiences that are beyond those even being dreamed about today.

Artificial intelligence may be needed to solve problems of the future that are beyond the capacity of human minds. People will be the programmers and organizers of projects for the intellectual computers which will satisfy human needs. At least a minimal level of control will almost certainly be built into future computers, but education and knowledge are the keys to such control. The topic of whether or not computers might someday develop a self-awareness and "take over" is discussed later in this book.

Artificial intelligence programs are designed to be as general as possible so that, given a program and the knowledge relevant to solving a problem, the computer should be able to work out a method of doing it. Researchers in artificial intelligence try to create programs that not only work out step-by-step methods for solving problems but also, once the method is defined, carry out the steps. Artificial intelligence researchers are trying to get computers to link common characteristics of separate facts.

Micromice that run mazes are some of the most appealing examples of computers that appear to exhibit a kind of artificial intelligence. These artificial rodents can "feel" their way and memorize the correct path after two tries in a maze. On the third run, Moonlight Special, the micromouse pictured on pages 19 and 20, can crawl from start to finish without making a wrong turn or bumping into a wall. Its "brain" is a micro-computer that completely maps the maze in two passes and

makes 33 decisions each time the gray, fiberglass animal runs a
20-foot-square maze.

Moonlight Special is just one of many electronic mice
designed for the Amazing Micro-Mouse Maze Contest in which
engineers ran their "toys" through an unknown maze by use of
the logic and memories within each mouse. Thousands of such
mice have run in trial contests from coast to coast in the United
States, and some participated in a national contest that was run
at a computer conference in New York.

Moonlight Special, the mouse in the picture, is the product
of about 500 hours of work by six engineers who "moonlighted"
to create it at the Battelle Pacific Northwest Laboratories. The
mouse's energy is supplied by a rechargeable battery pack that
frees it from wires and external power sources. It glides through
the maze on two wheels that are driven by its motors. The
motors rotate the wheels an exact distance for each pulse of
electricity, and the microprocessor counts the pulses to keep
track of the distance covered. Light beams are used to identify pathways in the maze, and the computer "brain" inter-
rupts the light beam and stops the mouse when it approaches
the walls.

The rodent's memory includes four small chips, each 1" by
1½", for the storage of information. Two chips contain
Moonlight Special's program, all the information it needs to
function and control its response under given conditions. It is
these chips, for example, that produce the signal needed to
make the mouse turn left when it encounters a wall either in
front of it or to the right side. When the battery pack is turned
off, information in the temporary microprocessor is erased.
Then Moonlight Special is ready to learn the course of the next
run.

"Moonlight Special," a micromouse, navigates the Amazing Micro-Mouse Maze. —Battelle Pacific Northwest Laboratories

"Moonlight Special" was made by six engineers who "moonlighted" to create this micromouse.                    *—Battelle Pacific Northwest Laboratories*

The goal of artificial intelligence to increase capability is especially interesting in the world of robots. A great deal of research in this field concerns adding "eyes," "hands," and "feet" (in the form of wheels) to make them function in more helpful ways. These machines may not look like the robots of science fiction, and they may not see the way people do, but they can recognize patterns and accomplish some amazing tasks.

Although some people feel that computers that think may cause nothing but trouble, most everyone who understands the progress in artificial intelligence is eagerly looking forward to the day when computers can solve an increasing number of the world's problems that cannot be solved by human beings.

# 2.
# THINKING MACHINE OR IDIOT COMPUTER?

People have been arguing for many years about whether or not computers are potentially intelligent machines. "Can a computer think?" has been asked again and again. A book called *The Thinking Machine* was published in 1962 to describe a "new breed of machine" known as the computer. These machines were described as among the most expensive necessities yet invented, costing hundreds of thousands of dollars apiece. Today anyone may own a personal computer costing just several hundred dollars that can "think" as well as one of the old giants. It balances the checkbooks, plans the menus, plays games with its owner, and is a good teaching tool for the children. One can program it with ease, and it communicates with the programmer to point out an error. The computer never makes a mistake, provided its electrical circuits are properly functioning. The error is always human. Sometimes the computer seems so smart that it is irritating—until one remembers that without the programmer the computer cannot do anything at all.

However, John Pfeiffer, the well-known author of *The*

*Thinking Machine* states, "of course computers think." Pfeiffer's reasoning is as follows: Computers do for the brain what other machines do for the muscles. Bulldozers do work and no one argues that point. They do not work without the help of a person, but they work. "Computers do think," he says. They do not store information or perform memory searches without the help of a programmer, but they do think.

Stanley L. Englebardt wrote a book called *Computers* that was published about the same time as *The Thinking Machine.* Under the title on the paperback edition one finds the following: " 'Thinking machines' and their fantastic abilities—from language translation to the exploration of space." In this case "thinking machines" is placed in quotation marks. In the chapter titled "Can They Think?" this author notes that no computer has come up with a totally original thought that was not first asked for through programming. But he also notes that many serious scientists believe that machines may be capable of going beyond their designers.

Some of today's computers possess a degree of originality. Certainly some computers simulate a portion of the human thinking process. In some areas, they outperform the human brain.

"Are computers a species?" asks John G. Kemeny, an outstanding computer expert who is co-inventor of the widely used computer language known as BASIC. In his book *Man and the Computer,* which was written a decade after the two books mentioned earlier, he considers the computer as to characteristics often attributed to living things and notes that they show ability to communicate, that they show individuality, and that some computers exhibit a sort of metabolism. He also suggests that a robot might exhibit metabolism, which is defined as the ability to perform a chemical change in matter to generate energy.

Computer-directed robots can be equipped with power cells and can be instructed to go to electric outlets periodically, plug themselves in, and recharge their batteries.

Living things have the characteristic of being able to reproduce. Industrial robots can, and do, reproduce themselves in factories. In the area of sense organs, some robots see and listen in a primitive sort of way. There is little question about their having locomotion.

Some of the above comparisons seem ridiculous to many people, but Dr. Kemeny states that there is no question in his mind about the intelligent quality of computers—because they could be programmed in such a way that they would do well on intelligence tests.

However, not everyone agrees how well computers might fare on intelligence tests. Many of today's experts still classify them as electromechanical idiots. They point out that intelligent animals developed their brains over a very long period of time compared with the time scale of the computer world. In some areas, computers are far ahead of human brains. While the computer calculates numerical problems much faster than the brain, the capacity of the brain for handling visual data is far superior to the computer's. A supercomputer that achieves the speed of 800 million, or even a billion, instructions per second is still inferior to the human brain, for the brain's cells do millions, or even billions, of operations simultaneously. However, many experts believe the speed of computers will surpass that of the human brain in this kind of activity very shortly. But can computers be programmed to use vision more efficiently or to reason? How much more intelligent will these machines become in the near future?

One of the problems in considering whether or not computers are intelligent is the confusion over a definition of intelligence. Even though everyone has some idea of what is meant by intelligence, it is difficult to be specific. Would you consider a 17-year-old who can speak some French, do college-level calculus, and play checkers and chess well enough to beat most of the people in town intelligent? Most people would, even before testing his or her qualifications against the dictionary definition.

According to *The Random House Dictionary,* intelligence is "the capacity for reasoning, understanding, and for similar forms of mental activity; aptitude in grasping truth, facts, meaning." Now instead of considering the 17-year-old, suppose a computer is the subject of this discussion. Do you still consider him, her, or it intelligent?

Many people who become upset at the idea of a machine being intelligent are quite willing to accept the idea of intelligence in a variety of animals. According to one definition of animal intelligence, it is "the ability to adapt to changes in environmental conditions through changes in behavior." On the basis of this definition, even a simple, one-celled animal shows some intelligence, for it moves away from some stimuli and toward others.

Many of the actions that humans consider intelligent in animals may be the result of inborn ingenuity. The behavior patterns of birds that fly long migratory routes and of insects that make slaves of other insects have long been thought to be written in their genes. However, Donald Griffin, in *Animal Thinking,* does not ask, "Do animals think?" He asks, "What do animals think about?" His theory poses new ideas about animal intelligence.

It seems obvious that many animals, especially mammals, can actually learn a great deal. Almost everyone is familiar with

The average chimpanzee can easily be taught a variety of skills.

*—Lincoln Park Zoo/Bud Bertog*

the tricks that can be taught to dogs and other pets. Cats are not exceptionally intelligent when compared to apes, but some cats learn to turn on a water faucet when they want a drink. A sea lion can be trained to blow horns in such a way that it plays *Yankee Doodle.* Actually, the sea lion has been trained to blow the horns in a certain order by being rewarded with fish after playing a proper note. Through a long series of rewarding desired behavior with a treat of fish, the trainer has taught the sea lion to play a tune that pleases people. However, the sea lion would play the horns in the same order even if the horns all made exactly the same sound.

The average chimpanzee can easily be taught to eat with a fork and to use tools such as a saw, hammer, and screwdriver. Chimps have been taught to count up to five and how to insert the pegs in toy puzzles. Some chimps learn the correct way to put square, round, and triangular blocks in the proper holes faster than very young children.

As long ago as 1925, studies showed that apes are reasonably intelligent. Experimenters suspended fruit so that the apes could not reach it. In such experiments, many apes carried a box to place beneath the fruit, stood on the box and reached the fruit. In one experiment an ape exhibited a behavior that was even more intelligent. The animal spotted a bunch of bananas outside his cage. After many tries, he inserted one bamboo shaft inside another to make a pole long enough to reach them.

In other experiments chimps have stacked boxes under suspended bananas and, when they still could not reach the bananas, have used a stick to knock them down. Psychologists point out that many three-year-old children cannot learn to stack blocks to build a tower. However, chimpanzees are usually considered to be about as bright as a three-year-old person.

Chimpanzees are usually considered to be about as bright as a three-year-old person.
*—Lincoln Park Zoo/Bud Bertog*

Some chimps have been taught to use computer consoles to communicate with humans and, in certain cases, with each other. Duane Rumbaugh, a researcher working at Yerkes Regional Primate Center, taught the chimp Lana to communicate with humans by punching out messages on a computer-like console to form 256 words and to use words in combination to release food from a vending machine and to obtain companionship or entertainment.

In testing any animal on a standard intelligence test, it is only fair to take into account the fact that the tests were designed to measure certain qualities in people. Christopher Evans in his popular book *The Micro Millennium* suggests that one use the number 1,000,000 as the average intelligent quotient for human beings rather than 100. Judging animals on such a scale, slow-learning humans would have an IQ of 999,970, and very, very bright ones would be in the 1,000,070 range. A dog or cat would rate about 300,000 to 500,000, and an ape might score in the 800,000 range. Evans rated the brightest of computers somewhere around 3000 on his scale, a position below the fish. He made this estimate in 1978, and he might well give computers a higher rating today. But even the smartest computer would rate well below the average person.

A computer is not intelligent or "clever like a fox," an animal that can do intuitive thinking, make bright guesses and leap to conclusions and determine all its own instructions without programming provided by another animal.

Some of the "smart" machines have been compared with toddlers who are learning to speak and stack blocks, but human capability for intelligence is so diverse that it is extremely difficult to measure.

The tests used to measure the mental ability of human beings include a variety of categories such as abstract reasoning, verbal reasoning, numerical reasoning, space relations and perception. Computers rate higher in some of these areas than in others, but they are improving in almost every way.

Computers have long rated high with regard to some of the characteristics that go with intelligence. Few would question the ability of a computer to make decisions based on information or the ability of a computer to solve problems. Some chess computers improve with every game, exhibiting an ability to learn from experience.

Many people who find it difficult to accept the idea that computers can exhibit intelligence are quick to emphasize that a computer can only do what it is told to do. Instructions must be stored in every computer in the form of a program. Today the program can include instructions for learning and adapting to the outside world. Computers that store a vast body of knowledge can be programmed to learn from their own experiences and to make decisions based on these experiences and their own stores of information. These computers can manipulate symbols to reach logical conclusions based on information provided by the programmers. But even the smartest computers are a long way from being able to understand the way humans do.

A famous test for computer intelligence was suggested by Alan Turing, an English mathematician, more than a quarter of a century ago. In this test, a person is in a room where there are two computer terminals. One terminal is connected to a human being and the other is connnected to a computer. The person performing the test does not know which terminal is connected with the computer and which is connected with the other person. He or she uses the terminals to type out questions that the person and the computer answer by machines that print the answers in an identical typeface. The person performing the test has the task of determining which is which.

A sophisticated computer might carry on a good conversation with the person who is to act as the judge in the Turing test. Executives have been known to mistake their computers for their associates. For example, a man and a woman are carrying on a conversation via a computer network. The man leaves the room without telling the woman and the computer continues to converse with her. A brief period may pass before the computer is recognized as not being her associate. However, this is not considered to be a true example of passing the Turing test. If the woman were alerted to the necessity of deciding whether or not she was talking to a person, she might have recognized the computer sooner.

Consider the Turing test in the context of a chess game. Peter J. Sandiford, director of operations research for Trans-Canada Air Lines, arranged an experiment in which two students played chess with computers when they thought they were playing with one another. The referees and the chess computers were together in a separate room, listening to the comments of the boy and girl players. The referees kept the score and helped to operate the computers. The charade reached its conclusion without either person suspecting the true nature of his or her opponent. The students were astonished when they were brought into the room with the robot chess players. They found it difficult to believe they had not been playing chess with each other.

Suppose a chess grand master cannot tell whether or not the opponent is a person or a computer? Would this be an example of passing the Turing test? International grand masters have occasionally lost to computers, but this is a limited display of machine intelligence.

Turing anticipated that his test would not be passed by machines before the beginning of the twenty-first century. To pass the test, a computer would have to store a huge amount of knowledge about the real world.

Since the beginning of the computer era, data and instructions have moved from a computer's memory through a single path to the central processing unit. The instructions are carried out by the processor, and the result is sent back to the memory. This is a step-by-step, or serial, approach. But the available processing power sets a limit to the amount of material that can be handled. Research in artificial intelligence, which needs huge amounts of memory capacity, has been hampered by the limits of computers. Bigger programs get smarter, but they also get slower.

The human brain provides important clues to solving some of the problems of making computers smarter. A number of computers are being developed to handle information with parallel processing. In this method, 1000 to 65,000 or more processors are doing calculations at one time. Dividing the work over lots of processors does speed things, but how should the processors be connected? If each task is parceled out to a different microprocessor, or self-contained computer on a chip, a traffic cop or ring master is needed so that the individual processors do not duplicate tasks or run into a bottleneck awaiting access to the computer's central memory. Many different researchers are exploring ways of connecting processors with the aim of building systems that model the intelligence of the human brain.

Computer experts have suggested that one think about the difference between serial and parallel processing in terms of a national election. In a serial arrangement, one person would vote at a time and it would take a tremendously long time to cast all the ballots. In reality, the action is like parallel processing. Many people vote at once, with processing power being distributed to individual states, counties, cities, and districts that simultaneously count and record the votes.

The human brain has a complex system of linking the information that it holds in storage. Think about how much information you would have to include in directions for teaching a child to ride a bicycle. You can instruct a person with just a few words. A similar computer program would not be so simple. And what about the problem of emotion? In some laboratories, artificial intelligence researchers are beginning to try to teach computers to deal with information that involves emotions, but most doubt that machines will ever "feel" very deeply.

Certainly, computers are far from being intelligent in the full sense. The nagging question about whether or not the machines will reach the point where they will become so intelligent that they will take over from man continues, but for all its amazing performances, the computer is still a dumb machine and humans can still pull the plug.

# 3.
# ON/OFF IS ALL
# THE COMPUTER KNOWS

In order to have some understanding of what is happening in the world of artificial intelligence, it helps to have a basic idea about how a computer functions and how computers are evolving.

Again and again one hears the expression, "The computer can do only what you tell it to do." In other words, a computer cannot do anything that has not been programmed into its memory. Even though a chess computer may play better chess than the person who designed the programs, the better game played by the computer is accounted for by its attributes of enormous speed and accuracy.

While many young children can write programs for computers, most adults find everything about computers very mystifying. Actually, a program consists of a set of instructions that causes it to run through a series of tasks. Only a computer program can tell a computer what to do, even though, as mentioned earlier, some sophisticated computers can be programmed to modify their own programs.

Computers have three main sections each dedicated to

perform a different function. There is a central processing unit that carries out logical and arithmetic tasks. This part is the organizer, the part that controls the sequence of all the operations.

A second section is the memory where information is stored. There are generally two types of information stored in the memory: the program, or instructions, to be carried out by the computer and the data upon which the program acts.

A third section is the input/output system, which enables the computer to interact with the user. There are many kinds of input and output devices. The keyboard and the card reader, which converts holes in punched cards into electrical impulses, are popular forms of input devices. Screens similar to those on television sets, printers, magnetic tape drives, and spoken voice are popular kinds of output devices. The output of a computer may be connected with data banks, where large amounts of information are stored and transferred to individual terminals in remote places.

All three sections described above are commonly known as hardware. Software is the term used for the set of computer programs and for other programming material associated with using the computer.

The basic building block of the computer is a switching device called a transistor. The smallest unit of information that a computer can use is one binary digit, represented by a single switch in an on or an off position. An electric light with its switch has been compared to a simple computer. The light switch can be either on or off and the light bulb tells you in which position the switch is: either on or off.

In the computer, too, switches or transistors respond to the presence or absence of electric current, and this presence or absence is controlled by switches. The central processor in a computer is a place where calculations are performed by literally thousands of transistor switches continually changing their on-off position.

A system that is only on or off is known as a binary system, one that has just two positions. You may be familiar with binary arithmetic, a system in which only two numbers are used, a 1 and a 0. A computer carries out calculations in binary

A system that is only on or off is known as a binary system.

*—Courtesy of IBM*

arithmetic. Switches are either on or off; a switch that is off can represent a 0. A row of switches that can turn off and on can represent a row of numbers based upon the binary representation of 1 or 0.

In computers, millions of individual operations can be carried out in one second, with this binary system as the basic building block. A binary digit is commonly called a bit and a sequence of adjacent binary digits, or bits, operated as a unit are called bytes. A byte is a basic unit of information stored in the computer and usually consists of eight bits.

Patterns of 1's and 0's can be used to represent more than numbers. Computers can represent one kind of thing in terms of another by allowing the numbers to represent letters, shades of color, speeds, weights, and an almost endless list of things. You are probably familiar with the Morse code that is used to represent letters. Computer codes are a much more flexible form of handling information than the "da dit" system.

More than a century ago, George Boole, the mathematician, worked out a system of algebra that is based on symbols which can be binary in character. Part of this mathematical language consists of elements that are either true or false and, as such, the algebra is logical in structure rather than arithmetic. Since the binary digits, 0 and 1, can stand for false and true respectively, a computer can be used to solve logical as well as numerical problems. This two-valued logic fits in beautifully with the way computers operate.

Another major contribution to the world of computers was made long ago by another mathematician, Charles Babbage. In fact, Babbage is often considered to have invented the computer. His strange looking "analytical engine" (although never completed) was the beginning of programmable computers. It had a set of input devices or methods by which he could

The "Babbage" calculator played a significant part in the history of today's complex computers.                    *—Courtesy of IBM*

feed numbers or instructions into it. It had an arithmetic unit or processor where the numbers were calculated, a control unit where certain tasks were completed in proper sequence, a memory where numbers could be stored waiting their turn to be processed, and an output mechanism. These are the five basic components of any computer.

The many columns of toothed wheels and the many rods that clanked in the Babbage machine were quite different from a modern computer, but this and other calculators played a significant part in the history of today's complex machines.

One characteristic runs through the development of computers as well as the popular simple computers that just handle numerical calculations, the hand calculators. That characteristic is increased speed and efficiency, achieved with a reduction in size. From the abacus, a manual device that is still used in some countries, to modern data processing machines, efficiency and speed are important. Today's computers are systems of machines the speeds of which are measured in microseconds (millionths of a second) or nanoseconds (billionths of a second). The human mind cannot imagine such speeds, but it may help to compare what a computer can do in the half second that it takes spilled coffee to reach the floor.

Within the time it takes coffee spilled from a pot on the table to reach the floor, a fairly large computer can debit 4200 checks to 630 bank accounts, *and* examine the electro-cardiograms of 210 patients and alert physicians in case of trouble, *and* score 315,000 answers on 6300 examinations, evaluating the effectiveness of the questions, *and* figure the payroll for a company with over 2000 employees, *plus* more chores.*

---

*Calculations courtesy C. D. Siegchrist, IBM Technical Editor.*

Early computers were large and slow.

*—Courtesy of IBM*

An old card sorter cost more than many of today's multi-purpose machines.

*—Courtesy of IBM*

---

The following experiment also may help you to have some understanding of the speed at which computers function. Time yourself as you multiply 3548 by 754. Did it take you a minute or so? How long does it take you to do this multiplication on a pocket calculator? How did you spend most of the time with

This electronic multiplier dates to 1946. *—Courtesy of IBM*

the calculator? Which answer do you think has a greater chance of being accurate, the handwritten one or the one from the calculator? If you could eliminate the time it took to turn on the calculator, push the buttons, and read the answer, you would reduce the time for this procedure so much that the remaining time used for the actual multiplication process is very small indeed. The very fact that computers can operate so accurately with what seems like instantaneous speed has been suggested as one reason so many people feel uncomfortable about these machines.

There is another trend in the history of computers. This is reduction in size. Long ago, the most complicated computers were called "giant brains," a name that may have had an influence on the people who resist the idea of artificial intelligence. In any case, the so-called giant brains really were very large computers. These computers were not only massive, they were comparatively slow.

Mark I, which was considered to be the world's first operational electromechanical computer, was unveiled in 1944 after five years of work by Harvard's Dr. Howard Aiken, with the help of IBM. It stood over eight feet tall and weighed five tons. In its 51 feet of length, it contained over 500 miles of wiring and almost a million different components. This machine could multiply two 23 digit numbers in six seconds.

I. J. Good and D. Michie were among the pioneers who developed the computer in the United Kingdom that many people believe "won the war" for the Allies because of its ability to crack the German codes. This computer, the Colossus, used 200 radio-type tubes, an almost unbelievably large number for the time. These could flip on and off like switches and could count thousands of times faster than could moving mechanical parts. The Colossus and the electronic computers that soon followed it were developed only to crack enemy codes.

An all-purpose computer that was built at the University of Pennsylvania and installed at the Aberdeen weapons proving ground in Maryland in 1947 contained 19,000 tubes, was as large as a six-room house, weighed 28 tons, and needed as much electricity as a small power station to operate it. Called ENIAC (Electronic Numeral Integrator and Calculator), this computer had to be rewired each time a new program was used. Soon after this, the world-famous mathematician John von Neumann introduced the concept of internally stored programs, an important step in the development of computers.

Many smaller, more efficient computers followed. By 1946, IBM vacuum-tube machines could multiply two 10 digit numbers in 1/40th of a second. By 1953 it took only 1/2000th of a second.

The new age of computers came with a revolutionary invention at the Bell Telephone Laboratories in 1947: the transistor. While in a vacuum tube electrons move through the open space that has been evacuated, in transistors, the electrons move through a solid crystal. This makes possible a great reduction in size and in the amount of energy needed to power the systems using them. Most transistors are made of silicon. Today the silicon chip is a well-known term.

The specially prepared silicon used is a semi-conductor, a material that will not conduct an electric current until the current rises to a certain level. When it reaches this point, the electricity suddenly flows through the silicon and the switch is on. This makes it an excellent material for computers.

Transistors can easily be connected to function in an on/off arrangement on silicon chips. With modern technology, the number of transistors on a chip has increased tremendously and the capacity of computers has increased along with this. Since computers are basically nothing more than a vast collection of electrical switches that turn off and on, a computer can be made to handle more information per second by increasing the number of switches. The more circuits, the more a computer can do.

In 1960, one transistor fit on a silicon chip. That is, the chip was the transistor. Its size was a square just about a half

*Above:* Part of a vacuum tube, a transistor, and a chip with 22 transistors.

*Bell Telephone Laboratories*

*Opposite:* A primitive transistor, 1947.          *Bell Telephone Laboratories* centimeter on each side. Ten years later, a thousand transistors could be squeezed into this tiny space. By 1980 a hundred thousand switching units could be squeezed onto a single chip, making one tiny piece of silicon more powerful than some of the early computers. Today's researchers are working toward a million circuits on a chip. While the quest for miniaturization continues, computers play an increasingly larger role in the lives of people, whether or not they realize it. From the chemical processing plant that an engineer operates from a remote site with a computer that monitors heat, light, weight, and humidity to the electronic games that entertain people of all ages, computers help to make life easier and more pleasant.

Reduction in the size of switches is one way to increase the capability of a computer. Another way is to make them turn on and off faster. A microprocessor, the computer's arithmetic system, is an electronic circuit on a chip in which the wires and the insulators are all formed together in a single block of silicon. This is known as an integrated circuit, a term used to distinguish it from earlier arrangements in which the transistors were made first and the connections were added by means of wires and solder. A grid of metallic strips on the chip is used to connect the transistors to other parts. A microprocessor connected to a control system and a memory system make a microcomputer.

Producing circuits on chips is a very intricate process since the "wiring" is so fine. Workrooms are surgically clean, for a tiny speck of dust would ruin a chip. A chip one quarter inch on the side may contain over 25 feet of wiring. Using one process, IBM can print the entire Bible, all 1250 pages of the

---

A memory chip in the eye of a needle.                    *—Courtesy of IBM*

Old and New Testaments, on a wafer 1½ inches square.

Not only can circuits be made unbelievably small, but they can be made to switch on and off at incredible speeds, measured in trillionths of a second. Signals travel through wiring at the rate of slightly less than 12 inches per billionth of a second, or per nanosecond.

Today's computer researchers are trying to create supercomputers that will be even faster and more powerful. The definition of supercomputers changes from time to time, but generally they are defined as the fastest computers available at any given time. The Cray 2, which was said to be the most powerful computer designed by early 1986, is potentially capable of a billion operations per second.

Many researchers need huge amounts of number-crunching power, power to do many small calculations at very high speed. For example, those who predict weather patterns, analyze geological data in their search for oil, and study the airflow around an entire airplane analyze tremendous amounts of statistical data. In March 1985, the National Science Foundation announced the establishment of supercomputer centers at Cornell University, Princeton University, the University of California at San Diego, and the University of Illinois at Urbana/Champaign. These four centers are the core of a network connecting about 30 other schools. Scientists can obtain time to use these supercomputers for their pet research projects, which vary from predicting the effect of earthquakes on bridges to designing computers that are a thousand times more powerful than the supercomputer they are using.

For many researchers, the next frontier is different from simply increasing the number-crunching power of conventional computers. They are searching for ways of making computers that can reason and learn.

# 4.

# MOVING TOWARD INTELLIGENT ROBOTS

Fashioning robots that would perform tasks to help people is an ancient dream. Perhaps the very earliest work in the search for artificial intelligence was the creation of mythical robots.

Although many people think of Frankenstein's monster when they picture a robot, the original in Mary Shelley's story was created before the word "robot" came into use. Many variations of the original story have kept it alive.

A very popular story that is much older than Frankenstein is the story of Golem, a robot-like creature made of clay. According to one version of this story, the chief rabbi of Prague created a creature in the year 1580 from clay of the local riverbank. He named it Joseph Golem and he made it for the purpose of spying on the enemies of the Jews. The rabbi, with the help of two assistants, formed it in the dead of night and, after proper incantations and prayers, implanted the name of God on the creature's forehead. It came alive!

Although Joseph Golem could not talk, the rabbi managed to make good use of it as a spy. When the robot was not busy with that task, it served as the rabbi's janitor. One day, the rabbi's wife asked Joseph Golem to bring water from the well without being specific about how much water. The creature brought more and more water until the rabbi was called from his devotions to bring the situation under control. There were many times when the "golem" was troublesome and at times, *it* appeared to be in control. This idea of losing control to robots is one that motivates some of the people who oppose research in the field of artificial intelligence. The rabbi was able to destroy the Joseph Golem, perhaps by removing the name of God from its forehead. However, the idea of a golem continued to be used in various stories, and in medieval Jewish legend, a golem was any automaton-like clay servant that was brought to life by means of a charm.

Mechanical dolls and other creatures that worked by mechanical means became popular in later years, and many of these were the subjects of stories in which they were made and destroyed by a variety of means. The stories of Pinocchio, the Emperor's Nightingale, Dorothy's adventures with the scarecrow and the tin woodman in the Land of Oz, Alice and the playing cards that came to life at the mad queen's party, the toy soldiers that marched at midnight in the Nutcracker Suite, and the Frankenstein monster continue to entertain people.

The word "robot" did not come into popular use until the early 1920's with the appearance of a play called *R.U.R. (Rossum's Universal Robots)* in which artificial zombie-like creatures took over the world. Although there are many definitions of robots today, they are generally described as creatures, or machines, that function under their own power and control.

---

This robot was built by Dr. Michael Freeman when he was 13 years old. His teaching robot, 2 XL, is popular with children.

*—Courtesy of Dr. Michael Freeman*

Robots in science fiction are ever popular, even though they are quite different from the robots that work for humans in the real world. In the past, many fictional robots were unpleasant or evil characters that gained control of humans, and it was common for people to think of these artificial creatures as dangerous. The robots of space fiction have done much to change the current feelings about robots, for they usually follow the three famous "Laws of Robotics." These were suggested back in the year 1950 by the author Isaac Asimov:

1. A robot may not harm a human being or allow a human being to come to harm through inactivity of the robot.
2. A robot must obey the orders or commands given to it by human beings unless these conflict with the first law.
3. A robot must protect itself at all times as long as such protection does not conflict with the first two laws.

The popular robots in the film *Star Wars* and many other fictional robots are law-abiding creatures. They are often very appealing in appearance and personality. Certainly they are much different from most of the actual robots that work in industry and are being developed in the laboratories of artificial intelligence researchers.

Some of the actual robots of earlier times were appealing, too. In the eighteenth century, mechanical figures of animals and humans were especially popular. These performed a series of actions that imitated real life. A model of a person dipped pen in ink and wrote on a pad. A flute player, the size of a human, played 12 melodies. Mechanical people danced and mechanical ducks drank and splashed in the water. They all followed specific programs of actions that were determined by a device similar to the mechanism contained in music boxes. This type of robot is sometimes called a "clockwork automaton."

In the modern world mechanical figures do not seem threatening, but in the eighteenth century they inspired discussions about whether or not machines can think. Many people found them disturbing, just as many people today are disturbed by the search for artificial intelligence. In the eighteenth century, some mechanical figures were accused of being the work of witches, and at least one designer of automatic people was arrested on the charge of witchcraft by the Holy Inquisition.

Many years later, in 1948, the British brain physiologist W. Grey Walter invented an appealing type of robot he called a "machina speculatrix," but which was popularly known as a tortoise or turtle. There were many of these turtles, but each was a metal box on wheels in which there were two "sense organs." One "sense organ" was a bank of photocells that looked in the direction in which the tortoise was steering. In the absence of light, the turtle kept going around in circles, but when a light shown on it, it moved toward the light. However, if the light were very bright, the turtle moved away from it.

The other "sense organ" in the mechanical turtles was the shell, or box that housed the internal equipment, which, since it looked somewhat like a turtle, was responsible for giving them this popular name. If a turtle bumped into something, the shell detected this and the turtle moved along a random path until it cleared the obstacle.

One of the most interesting behaviors of the original turtle and its many "children" was the way these mechanical creatures returned to their "hutches" when their batteries needed recharging. Grey Walter placed battery chargers in the corners of the room, where the turtles could connect themselves when the batteries were low. Here they could plug in and "feed."

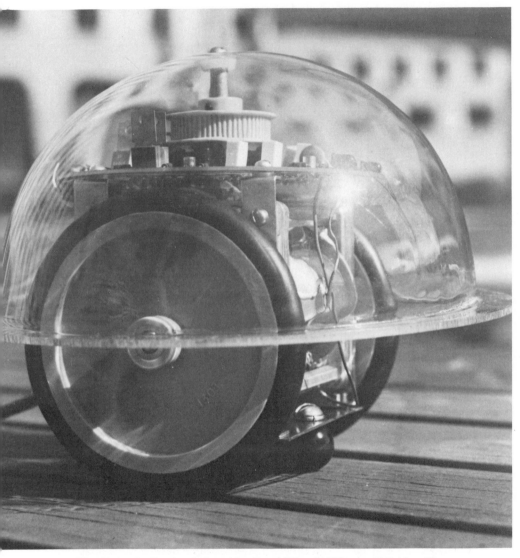

The Terrapin Turtle, designed by Dan Hillis of MIT's Artificial Intelligence
Laboratory, is used in schools and laboratories throughout the world.
                                        *—Courtesy of Terrapin, Inc.*

One of the purposes for building the turtles was to study the electrical activity of the brain. They also served the purpose of making people question whether or not they were "beings," since they had senses that could detect a stimulus and respond to it. They spawned numerous offspring, including the computer turtles that have been used in some recent teaching situations.

A robot turtle, the Terrapin Turtle, designed by Dan Hillis of Massachusetts Institute of Technology's Artificial Intelligence Laboratory, is being used by schools, colleges, universities, and research laboratories around the world. It is a computer-controlled device that has blinking eyes, beeps in two tones, draws with a pen, and moves on two separately controlled wheels. Most important, the Terrapin Turtle has a sense of touch. It provides a wide variety of learning opportunities as well as recreation.

Modern teaching robots take many forms, and some of the more exciting and smarter robots will be discussed in another chapter.

While scientists are searching for ways to make robots more intelligent, many dumb, low-level robots have been invading industry. For some processes, the machines do not have to be very sophisticated, but they appear intelligent compared with mechanical figures of former times. Consider the robots that work at the Roundtree Chocolate factory in England. They have two arms which give them the ability to pick up two pieces of candy at a time and place them in boxes. The most amazing thing about them is their speed. These robots work at the rate of two pieces of candy every second. The robots work tirelessly, never stopping for a coffee break. No worker ever stayed on this job in the chocolate factory for more than two years. The new workers never get bored, nor are they ever absent because of illness, vacation, or lack of transportation.

The Terrapin Turtle moves on two separately controlled wheels and has a
sense of touch. —*Courtesy of Terrapin, Inc.*

Robot mailmen are often speedier than the office mailmen, who stop to chat with people when they make their rounds. To some of the people who watch them, the robots seem rather bright. Suppose you are walking down the hall in an office building and a robotic mail cart comes along the hall on its way to delivering and collecting mail at your office and the others on your floor. You decide to see what happens if you stand in its way. The robot hits you with a gentle bump and waits until you step aside. You continue on your way and the robot continues on its way. This is just what it was programmed to do in case of such an emergency. In some ways it does not seem at all stupid, even though its computer "brain" is rather simple. It must only control a few functions, such as stop, start, turn, and beep horn. "Blue Eyes," a government-employed mail cart, has two twinkling lights on in front when it is operating, and like many other computer controlled carts, is a popular member of the office staff.

Many industrial robots do their jobs more efficiently and produce better results than people did in the same kind of work. Thousands of them are working in jobs that are hard, dangerous, or just boring. They don't mind working in places that are hot, freezing cold, dusty, or dangerous. They don't ask for overtime or care how long they work. Their "up time" is about 95% compared with that of human workers at 75%.

The industrial robot pictured on page 61 welds a base assembly that will hold computer parts. The robot welds 44 two-inch seams from a variety of angles in less than 12 minutes. It took 45 minutes for a human to weld this same kind of assembly.

Robots weld, load, and unload hot and heavy metal forms into machines that stamp them into a variety of shapes. And they do their jobs well. Robot car painters do a better job than people. General Motors expects to be using 1500 robot painters by the year 1990.

You might find it rather awesome to watch a robot at work. Its arm moves through the welding operation with a certain amount of grace, imitating the human arm and hand with a wide radial motion that seems too effortless and powerful. But even the most sophisticated robot hands cannot approach the complexity of the human kind.

The robot that replaces about a dozen workers at the Chesebrough-Pond's thermometer plant protects people from the possibility of mercury poisoning. Working in an isolated

3. Combined hydraulic/electrical power unit built to machine tool quality and standards.

ELBOW EXTENSION

SHOULDER SWIVEL

YAW

ARM SWEEP

PITCH

ROLL

2. Advanced ACRAMATIC computer control with solid-state IC electronics.

1. Jointed-arm robot—can be remotely controlled and located at any attitude.

This diagram of an industrial robot clearly shows the parts that add to its agility and versatility.                    *—Courtesy of Cincinnati Milacron*

This robot welds 44 two-inch seams in less than 12 minutes—almost a quarter of the time it would take a human being to weld the same assembly.

—*Courtesy of Cincinnati Milacron*

room, its computer brain guides it through a seven and one-half minute, 394-step program in which it works with two dozen different boxes. The robot follows a simple routine of lowering a box full of thermometers into a tank of hot water, transferring them into a tank of cold water, and placing them in a centrifuge. The purpose of all this is to squeeze out any air bubbles that might be present in the mercury that measures temperature. These would interfere with the accuracy of the thermometers.

Many factory workers who have been replaced by robots consider them helpers and are glad to let the robots do the unpleasant and dangerous jobs. Welding cars and spraying paint are ideally done at temperatures hotter than a human can stand.

Industrial robots perform tasks that are hard, dangerous, or just boring for the ordinary person. This robot is polishing sinks.        —*Courtesy of ASEA*

The picture on page 64 shows one of a variety of things that robots do today. Robots can spot weld auto bodies in eight places at once. They can lift and transfer 50-pound loads three times as fast as men. But they are still stupid machines. They need not be a threat so long as workers replaced are put into better or more interesting jobs. Even though the robots are vulnerable to sabotage, there have been no workers who have exhibited violence of the kind demonstrated by the followers of Edward Ludd, who physically attacked early machines of the industrial revolution. Luddites, as they were called, were concerned both for the workers who were being displaced by machines, and upset about the new technology. Technical innovations have long been feared and hated.

Many workers today are fond of the robots that help in industry, on farms, and in health care. Some of the robots are given names by their human co-workers and when "Clyde the Claw" broke down at an automobile stamping plant, it was given a get-well party. There are questions about how long this attitude will continue as the robot revolution, now in its infancy, moves ahead at a rapid pace. In the automobile industry, for example, robots are taking on an increasingly large number of jobs.

Driverless carts, called automated guided vehicles, can replace human-operated forklifts. They can deliver parts to assembly lines under computer control, following wire paths that are embedded in the floor. Automobile underbodies, side frames, and roof panels are temporarily assembled by humans by inserting small metal tabs into slots, much the way toy cars are put together. Then the cars move to an automatic welding station. When one reaches a robot, such as Robotgate, the body that is tucked together is clamped into exact position by 10 robots that apply 80 welds in 50 seconds. The entire body shell

Some industrial robots can weld auto bodies in eight places at once.

*—Courtesy of ASEA*

is put together in exactly the right alignment, eliminating any human error. Then, the car moves to another position where 44 robots apply additional structural welds.

Next, robots install the doors, and here, a machine vision system gets the door in the right place the first time. This is a more intelligent robot, of the kind discussed in the next chapter. Another robot with vision inspects the car and compares it with a mathematical model stored in the computer memory. If the car passes inspection, it goes on to the paint shop.

Now, a dozen robots spray sealant material on about 65% of the body seams and joints of the automobile. After this it is placed in a module where robots select the proper paint from 16 different colors according to the information they receive from the central data base at the plant. Paint robots cover the outside of the car with a colored base coat, and then hydraulic arms in the floor open the hood and the doors so the robots can spray inside. Excess paint is blown through the floor gate into water that is moving below. At the next station, paint robots spray on two clear coats of paint to make the glossy finish. Now the car travels through an infrared oven, where the paint is cured. Robots can paint 60 car bodies an hour, almost a thousand cars in one day.

From 40% to 60% of the robots at work in the United States are used by the automobile industry. Estimates of the number of industrial robots in the United States vary greatly, but many people believe the number will triple by the end of the century. Japan's robots far outnumber those in use in the United States.

The Zama factory in Japan, which is 97% automated, builds cars with very little human help. Its daily output of 1300 cars needs only 67 people per work-force shift. Japan's robot factory can work 24 hours a day with very little human participation.

The world's first robot system used to check car body integrity.

*—Courtesy of ASEA*

Here, long rows of industrial robots that look somewhat like birds make other robots like themselves. At night, they work in dim light, for they are blind, and only the human supervisors must be able to see to spot trouble. Sixty robots in this factory are capable of producing 60 new robots in 20 days.

Robots can work on objects both large and small. For example, they can insert and screw tiny light bulbs into the dashboard of an automobile. They can sort tomatoes, small machine tools, and a large number of other objects. Robots are being trained to shear sheep and pluck chickens. Consider the versatility of a robot that can write its name on the blackboard, then erase it , then write it again. One continued this pattern for hours on end at a recent robotics show, but it was just a dumb robot.

Teaching these robots to work is the responsibility of humans. There are three typical ways of programming these so-called "first generation" or low-level robots. "Lead through" is a method in which the operator guides the robot through the orientation and locations that are desired by means of a remote control "teach box" and imprints a pattern on its computer memory. "Walk through" is a method by which the robot is physically guided through the desired motions by a person. These are recorded and played back to the robot. The third method is known as "plug in." Here the robot operates through the use of a prerecorded program without the use of manipulation. "Plug in" programming is faster and a whole library of programs can be stored for future use. However, more problems arise when this method is used because of slight variations.

"First-generation" robots can do a variety of jobs, not just a repetition of one job as did the early robots that capped bottles. Since they can be programmed to work in different ways, they seem more intelligent than the "push and put" kind of machine—but they are still not very high on the brightness scale when measured against "second generation" robots.

Here is an example of a low-level robot making a mess of its job: It is working away performing a sequence of movements that result in the welding of identical pieces of metal. Another pair of pieces is presented to the robot, but this time they are in different positions from the usual ones. The robot is not bright enough to notice this, so it proceeds to weld them, putting the welds in the wrong place.

One of the applications of the search for artificial intelligence is to make smarter robots.

# 5.

# COMPUTERS THAT
# SEE AND FEEL AND TOUCH

A surface-roving vehicle lands on the moon and navigates a narrow path between two craters, independent of human control. Its computer brain has been programmed to send information back to earth and its computer-instructed sense organs help the robot to find its path. Suddenly, a moonquake changes the surface, and the robot slides down the side of a crater. It is intact but disoriented until it "looks around." The robot's vision enables it to compare the present location with the path above by examining the patterns of features such as boulders, mountains, and the sides of the crater. The robot compares this scene with the description of surroundings made shortly before it fell. It climbs up the crater wall to its original position and scoops up some sand in its mechanical hand. This is not the description of a robot in science fiction or one planned for 20 years from now, but of one that might be at work soon.

Robots with vision are already at work. At Texas Instruments Corporation, for example, camera-assisted robots

This Mars surface robot may operate for two years and travel about 1000 km performing experiments automatically and sending information back to earth. *—Jet Propulsion Laboratory*

inspect glowing diodes that are to light the numbers in pocket calculators. Humans could do this kind of inspection for only about two hours before all the lights would look alike to them. Robot "eyes" don't get tired and they do their work well.

As early as 1980, six robots—three sighted and three blind—went to work without the help of a human to assemble a motor that had as many as 50 parts. Of course, humans had done the programming of the robots beforehand.

Researchers long have been working toward smarter robots. They know that if a robot is going to be smarter than a simple manipulator, it must be able to respond to its environment. In addition to having arms that are jointed, claws that work like fingers, and computer brains, it needs to "see," "touch," or detect things in some other way.

Picture a robot arm reaching into a bin for a part that is needed for the next step in assembling a motor. The bin is full of different kinds of parts. How will the robot know which part to choose?

Television cameras that are positioned near the robot feed information to its computer brain, which has memorized the images of objects that the robot is processing. When the correct object is recognized, the computer calculates its distance and orientation and moves the robot's arm so that it will grip the right piece. This is a second generation robot, a robot with vision that can respond to its environment.

The first industrial robots with vision that made their way into factories can be compared to people with very bad eyesight. They see the world around them as a series of blurs. Such robots are valuable only for carrying out simple jobs such as picking up some items and putting them down at a certain place.

Robots with better vision have been developed and now gradually are joining older robots in the labor force. Some of these are so efficient that they can distinguish different sizes and species of fish that have been brought up in a fish net and can use their mechanical arms to separate the fish into bins. Some people say such robots sound magical and that they are scary. But the people who train such robots know that they can only see what they have been taught to recognize.

The Univision system is "trained by showing." Pictures of the sample parts that will be seen are made by the camera and records of these are stored in the computer memory. By combining a special robot with a vision system, the machine can measure, identify, and characterize stationary parts. In addition to this, it can do the same for randomly moving parts and make a variety of automatic inspections.

Autovision II, shown on page 73, is another system that may be used to inspect, identify, count, sort, position, and orient parts. It rejects defective parts, too. A random assortment of parts is presented at rates of up to 360 parts per minute, and information about each part is compared with information in the computer's memory to determine whether that part should be used.

Researchers who are trying to teach computers to see have gained new respect for human vision. Many of them believe that they underestimated the problem because it is so easy for people to see. But consider that the human retina has 100 million rods and cones to detect light and that its layers of neurons perform

---

Autovision II is a system used to inspect, identify, count, sort, position, and orient parts. It also rejects defective parts.     *—Courtesy of Automatrix, Inc.*

about 10 billion calculations per second. Although it was not so difficult to use tricks of lighting to heighten the outlines of objects so computers could identify them, the grays of the real world and the parts that the brain fills in are stumbling blocks for machine vision. Can you see two triangles in the diagram on page 75? Is the second triangle really there?

Scientists are trying to tease secrets from the brain, but they still have much to learn about how a person sees. The parallel processing mentioned on page 33 is one of the approaches that machine vision experts are exploring. Some are trying to understand how the brain fills in missing parts or parts that are indistinct. Others are concerned with surfaces, texture, colors, and shadings.

Dr. Patrick H. Winston of Massachusetts Institute of Technology is trying to teach a computer to recognize a cup when it sees one. When he points the TV-camera eye at an array of objects, the machine can pick out a cup even if it is an unusual-looking one with legs or bumps. Dr. Winston is pleased with the computer's performance, but he is quick to point out that a young child could do the same.

At the University of Rochester, Professor Nicholas George has built a machine that can tell the difference between a cat and a dog. First, it examines labeled pictures of dogs and cats. Then a laser illuminates each picture reflecting the bright and dark tones in it in differing degrees. A photodetector in the machine measures varying intensities of the reflected light, and a pattern of electronic signals is sent to the computer's memory. This process is repeated again and again. In this way, the computer learns which pattern represents a dog and which represents a cat, although it does not really understand the meaning the way humans do. While this is an example of computer vision growing sharper, this field is still in its infancy.

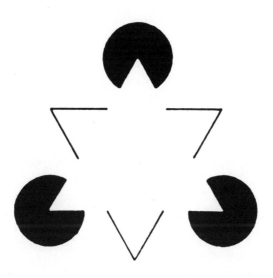

Do your eyes see the missing parts?

Most computer vision today is not patterned after human vision, but some valuable results of teaching computers to see have already entered the real world. This is the way some of robot vision is accomplished: A black and white picture can be divided into squares, and a binary number can be assigned to each square representing the shade of gray. You can get some idea of how shades of light and dark can be translated into a series of 1's and 0's for computer use by examining the diagrams on the opposite page.

Think about the scoreboard at a football stadium. Letters and numbers are made by lighting certain bulbs in a grid and keeping some bulbs dark. In computer vision, similarly, each character can be converted into an electronic grid of light and dark spots, and the pattern can be recognized.

Computers have been reading letters and numbers for more than 25 years. Consider the wide use of computers that read zip codes in the post office. Perhaps you shop at a store that uses the bar codes on packages at the checkout counter. Some cameras can catch the bar code when a package is in any position—the clerk does not have to find the code on the corn flakes package and place the code in a special position so the machine can read it.

A machine can read a printed or typed number or letter but reading handwriting is more difficult. Have you ever wondered why some address forms instruct you to place letters and numbers in small blocks? The computers that are used for these forms can read block letters and numbers when the letters are the proper size and have sufficient separation.

You can get some idea of the difficulties involved in computer vision by forming  a picture of a scissors in your mind. Now, think about how a scissors looks on a table when

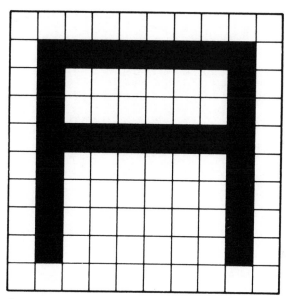

A black and white picture can be divided into squares, and shades of light and dark can be translated into a series of 1's and 0's for computer use.

*—Courtesy of Peter Kugel and* On Computing *magazine*

| 0 | 0 | 0 | 0 | 0 | 0 | 0 | 0 | 0 | 0 |
|---|---|---|---|---|---|---|---|---|---|
| 0 | 1 | 1 | 1 | 1 | 1 | 1 | 1 | 0 | 0 |
| 0 | 1 | 0 | 0 | 0 | 0 | 0 | 1 | 0 | 0 |
| 0 | 1 | 0 | 0 | 0 | 0 | 0 | 1 | 0 | 0 |
| 0 | 1 | 1 | 1 | 1 | 1 | 1 | 1 | 0 | 0 |
| 0 | 1 | 0 | 0 | 0 | 0 | 0 | 1 | 0 | 0 |
| 0 | 1 | 0 | 0 | 0 | 0 | 0 | 1 | 0 | 0 |
| 0 | 1 | 0 | 0 | 0 | 0 | 0 | 1 | 0 | 0 |
| 0 | 1 | 0 | 0 | 0 | 0 | 0 | 1 | 0 | 0 |
| 0 | 0 | 0 | 0 | 0 | 0 | 0 | 0 | 0 | 0 |

Can you see the connecting rod in this picture? The dark is mostly 2's and 3's while the light connecting rod is mostly 6's and 7's.

—Courtesy of General Motors Research Laboratories

you look at it from above. Suppose you were to stoop so that your eyes were level with the tabletop. How different it would look. But no matter how many ways you look at the scissors, you recognize it. On the other hand, for machine vision, making an object recognizable from all angles is a complex task.

When a computer's camera looks at an object and transmits large numbers of dots to the computer, these are transformed into binary code that depends on the light intensity at each point in the picture. On page 78 is a picture of a connecting rod that has been converted into numbers by a computer at the General Motors Research Laboratories. The range from dark to light has been limited to the numbers 0 to 9, which makes it easier for you.

To make the picture clearer, the digital picture is processed by an "edge finding" computer program. It is not as good as a photograph, but it is clear enough to be recognizable. If a robot can see where a part is, it can pick it up.

Some artificial intelligence experts believe that eventually a robot will be able to recognize objects it has never seen before by working out the meanings of shapes in much the way a person's brain can reach conclusions about objects he or she has never seen before.

Predictions of what robots can do when they have a better sense of touch encourage researchers to imitate the human body, too. Robots with microswitches that close when the hand or arm encounters an object are already in use. And there are strain gauges that measure the force that a robot's hand is exerting on the object it touches. Suppose a part that is needed for assembling a motor is not in exactly the right place. A strain gauge could alert the robot's computer, which could send commands to correct the position.

Installing a sense of touch may be an easier way of getting a robot to recognize an object and to handle it properly than providing it with vision. Certainly, this seems an easier route for some tasks. Dr. Melvin W. Siegal and Dr. Gregory M. Toto at Carnegie-Mellon University in Pittsburgh are experimenting with a plastic "skin" that has a large number of pressure-sensitive dots in it. Each sensor has its own microprocessor, which relays signals to a host computer for analysis. A complex system enables the device to "understand" a picture of the object.

Another approach to robot-touch engineering is being explored at the University of Florida in Gainesville. Here, Gale Neville and Robert Patterson are working with a sensor that mimics the ridges of a human fingerprint. When it is rubbed across a surface, the ridges create vibrations. A small sensor picks up the vibrations and sends them to a computer, where they are analyzed. In addition to identifying grades of sandpaper and recognizing in which direction the slot in the head of a screw is pointing, this sensor can read Braille.

These are just two examples of the ways in which scientists are developing a sense of touch in robots. Many different approaches are being explored in laboratories, where researchers continue to try to make robots smarter.

Someday, second generation robots that can see and feel may be set loose in large airports, or other places where there are large open spaces, at times when they are not busy. Imagine a large robot vacuum cleaner or polisher moving around without a human to guide it. The computer defines the room's boundaries and guides it to clean everywhere. Optical sensors prevent the machine from bumping into walls and furniture or any person who happens to walk in front of it.

Although second generation robots are sometimes called intelligent robots since they are able to acquire specific data concerning their work space and to react accordingly, it is the third generation robots that are seen in artificial intelligence laboratories. Third generation robots can sense the environment and perform a sequence of actions for which they have not been explicitly programmed.

Someday robots may irrigate fields, using exact knowledge of the conditions that exist and the needs of the crops. They also may plow fields, harvest crops, and perform a wide variety of other jobs, releasing the farmer for more important duties and allowing more time for recreation. Agriculture is just one of many areas where robots can make life easier for people.

Even today, large numbers of robots that see and feel are beginning to change the way people live. If you visit a library where a machine is reading to a blind person, you may feel that tomorrow already is here.

A television camera positioned near this robot enables it to locate a part on a conveyor belt. *—Courtesy of General Motors Research Laboratories*

# 6.
# TALKING, LISTENING, AND UNDERSTANDING STORIES

Teaching computers to read aloud, and do it well, is an extremely complex task, but thanks to artificial intelligence research, hundreds of reading machines are doing just that. Picture a 12-year-old blind boy as he is given a book of his choice. He places a page face down on the Kurzweil Reading Machine at his public library. When he presses a button, the reading machine tells the boy what it sees in a pleasant, slightly accented baritone voice. He listens to page after page until the book is finished, then he chooses another book. Most printed materials are not available in Braille or in Talking Books, so it is no wonder that this boy is spending much of his time at the library. Through the use of sophisticated computers that can read and talk, many new sources of education, entertainment, and culture are available to the blind and those physically handicapped who could not make use of printed materials in the past.

Reading machines are used by thousands of blind and visually handicapped people between the ages of 5 and 82 in over 500 locations worldwide. Unfortunately, expense limits the number of machines that are available—but a growing number are being placed in public and university libraries, schools for the blind, rehabilitation centers, federal and state agencies, and private corporation libraries.

Kurzweil reading machines help in a variety of ways. For example, a graduate student at Illinois Institute of Technology reports using a reading machine to help with texts and journals that were not available on tapes. The student, who has dyslexia, always had trouble reading. His vision is good, but his brain sometimes reverses letters, mixes syllables, or skips over words and lines. By placing one copy of a text on the Kurzweil Reading Machine so that he can listen to it while he follows along visually from another copy, he has less trouble processing information.

Reading machines have been gaining wide use among publishers, linguists and legislators who use them to read documents and store the information that they read in conjunction with computers. For example, the University of Texas uses one to record legal cases and make them available on computers to students who search for precedents. A publisher of large-print editions for the visually impaired uses a reading machine to record the contents of books making it easier for reprinting by computers. Linguists scan material written in languages such as Somale, Azerbaijaini (a Turkish dialect), Slovenian, and Mayan Indian. Through the use of these computers that depend on artificial intelligence, linguists are working at the University of Pennsylvania on an experimental project funded by the Defense Department. They aim to develop computer programs with which to create large computerized language files, to write other programs that will help analyze languages and help create grammars and dictionaries, and to expand computer-based language instruction.

The Kurzweil Reading Machine for the blind consists of three compact units. At the left is the user's keyboard. The scanner, with its glass top on which books or papers are placed, is here shown positioned on the separate computer control unit.     *—Courtesy of Kurzweil Computer Products*
*A Xerox Company*

People who use the reading machines have access to a wide variety of materials because the machine can recognize 300 different varieties of type and can read the print on various colors and qualities of paper. Computers in the machines convert the printed pages into spoken English at a rate as fast as 250 words a minute. This is twice as fast as ordinary human speech. Adjustments can be made for slow readers and fast readers or to produce the speed that any person wants for the kind of material that is being read.

Learning to use the reading machine takes only a few hours. You place the page that is to be read face down on the glass surface of the scanner. Then you activate a separate hand-sized control panel that causes the reading machine to locate the first line of the text automatically. It begins scanning the page, and within a few seconds, an electronic voice can be heard reading the material.

Children quickly master the Kurzweil Reading Machine's controls.

*—Courtesy of Kurzweil Computer Products*
*A Xerox Company*

New models of the reading machines allow for voice listening preferences. Controls let users vary the voice that is reading to them by adjusting the intensity of the "s" sounds, voice quality (resonance), and how low or high the pitch is. If you instruct it to do so, the machine will skip ahead in the text or return to an earlier part of the material that you are reading.

Reading machines are not new, but what is new is the way the Kurzweil Reading Machine reads and talks. Some earlier models were slow because the reader had to wait for the computer to search for the word stored in its memory bank. Others could read only a limited number of kinds of type.

The Kurzweil machine uses an advanced form of computer that enables the scanning system to recognize the letters of the alphabet in almost all printed materials. It uses a system called omni-font optical character recognition, where there is a search for the properties of a letter. For example, the letter "A" may be stored as many different combinations of its features, and these are analyzed to make certain that it is always read as "A." Certain characteristics are common to individual letters even in various types. The letter "A" has a concave area at the base and a loop at the top. The top is a completely closed area of white with extensions at the "west" side and "east" side.

Imagine the difficulty of programming a computer to recognize 300 kinds of type for each letter of the alphabet in both upper and lower case. Making it more complicated is the fact that some letters are poorly printed. The machine can compare a poorly printed letter "A" with well printed "A's" in the same material and recognize the letter for what it is meant to be.

Only after letters are recognized does the machine begin the comparatively simple process of converting the letters, numbers, and words into spoken English. The reading machine records the images that the camera takes from the printed page at the rate of 500 per second. A device on the back of the camera converts each image into electronic signals that the computer translates into characters. It groups these into words and sentences. Now the second part of the process, the talking part, begins. The computer processes pronunciation and articulation, reading with sensitivity to even such fine points as differences in the sound of "e" in the word "red" and the sound of the "e" in the word "reed."

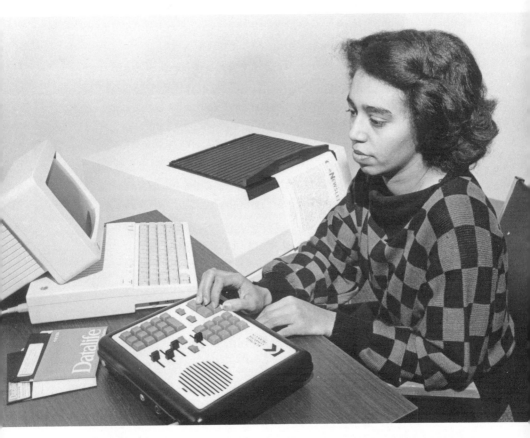

The Kurzweil Reading Machine can serve as an input or output device for a wide range of electronic, data processing, and Braille systems. Here it is used in conjunction with a microcomputer and Braille printer to convert print to Braille.

*—Courtesy of Kurzweil Computer Products*
*A Xerox Company*

Even though a "talking" computer is extremely complex, on the whole, it is much easier to design a machine that speaks than it is to design one that listens. Researchers remark that, in this respect, computers are much like humans, for they, too, are better at talking than they are at listening. Scientists have been exploring automatic recognition of natural speech for at least 40 years.

Most listening computers have limited vocabularies, but some of these may soon be useful to wide segments of the population in air traffic reservations and telephone directory assistance where limited vocabularies can be used. Some computers can understand a cross section of American speech, including some foreign accents and regional dialects from North to South and coast to coast.

IBM research scientists have developed an experimental speech recognition system that quickly and accurately recognizes spoken English sentences. Words, phrases, and sentences appear on the computer screen as the individual speaks. The IBM system includes an acoustic processor that digitizes the sound waves as they arrive at the microphone, and a decoder that analyzes the digitized waveform using two models. A language model produces information about which words are most probable in relation to other words in the sentence. An acoustic model produces information about which words are most probable given particular sounds.

This system can recognize sentences composed from a 5,000 word vocabulary and it identifies more than 95 percent of the spoken words correctly. One of the advantages of the IBM system is its speed: it can correctly recognize and transcribe speech almost as fast as the words are spoken. This system can train itself to recognize a person's voice by listening to the user read a brief text. During the training session, a short pause is required between words. But once the system is trained, words,

A speech recognition system trains itself to recognize a person's voice by listening to the user.

*—Courtesy of IBM*

---

phrases, and sentences appear on the workstation screen as the individual speaks. The resulting letter or memo may be edited by voice or keyboard.

The IBM recognition technique functions by determining the degree of similarity between the speech and the words in its vocabulary, as well as the probability that they would be used with other words in the sentence. It can distinguish between "to," "do," and "through" because they are pronounced differently and between "to," "too," and "two" based on surrounding words.

A number of speech recognition systems have been developed for special uses. Kurzweil Applied Intelligence is

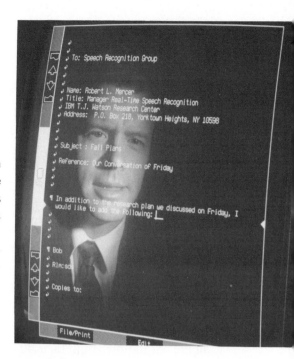

IBM's speech recognition system (below) allows a person to create office documents such as letters and memos by voice. Words, phrases, and sentences appear on a computer terminal screen as the individual speaks. The enlargement of the screen (right) shows the type of document that can be obtained by using this system.

*—Courtesy of IBM*

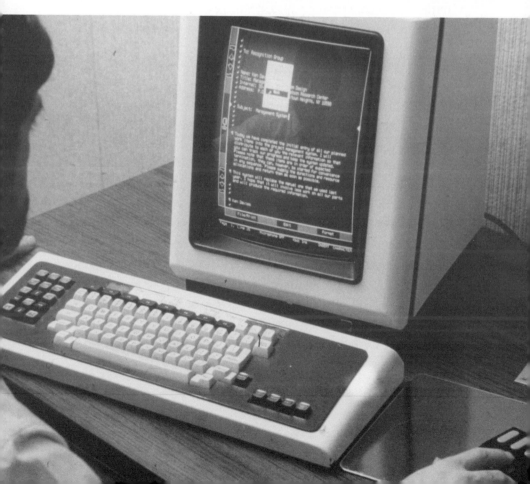

working to perfect a computer that will turn the spoken word into the written word with a shoe-box-sized device that connects to a personal computer. This system can fill in forms and write simple reports, but its vocabulary is far from the 100,000 words many adults know.

Although many speech recognition systems recognize only the voice they trained with, and although one must speak slowly for most speech recognition devices, such sophisticated "talk-writers" will be welcomed by many office workers.

Although progress is being made in teaching computers how to listen and respond, there is still much to be learned before you can hope to talk to a computer the way the space traveler spoke to Hal in *2001: A Space Odyssey.* However, it is conceivable that talking computers could be used in the future in space to monitor entire robot construction crews. The computers would act as go-betweens between humans and robots to guide construction of manufacturing plants and large space platforms.

One of the reasons for the difficulty in communicating directly with a computer is the fact that people use far more information than just sound waves in order to understand what they hear. Programming a computer to "understand" word sequences involves more than just the relationship of words. It involves knowledge and reasoning about the nature of the real world.

Scientists at a number of artificial intelligence centers are directing their research toward the goal of supplying background so that computers can draw inferences. The human brain does this so easily that one is seldom aware of it. For example, you may remark that you have a scratchy throat and had to go to two stores before you got relief. Almost everyone knows that you went to drug stores or places that carried medication, but a computer never had a sore throat. Nor has a computer ever been in a drug store.

At Yale University's Artificial Intelligence Project, computer scientists have programmed their machines to read stories and respond to them, with some rather amazing results. The project, under the direction of Dr. Roger C. Schank, is based on first understanding how people think and then making computers more intelligent by following the human model. They believe that people are the best models of intelligent behavior and they emphasize the fact that people are good at predicting the content of what they will hear. People are not good at remembering large numbers of words. This makes it most practical for them to begin processing a sentence before it is finished.

New work in understanding natural language uses a different approach from the early work. About 20 years ago, many scientists were very excited about the idea of using computers to make translations from one language to another.

Early translation programs did most of their changing from one language to another by simple word-for-word substitution. About 80% of the translation could be done by storing a large number of words in a computer's memory along with a number of rules dealing with grammar and relationships. The machine could come up with a translation that might be tolerated if a human editor could later work it over. Some of the mistakes that the computers made are famous. For example, "The spirit is willing but the flesh is weak" was translated into the Russian text and then the text was retranslated back into English as "The wine is agreeable but the meat is spoiled." "Out of sight, out of mind" was translated into the Russian equivalent of "Blind and insane." These are just two examples that show that languages are filled with expressions based on special meaning.

There were a host of difficulties in machine-language translations. It seems evident that a large vocabulary stored in the memory of a computer along with detailed rules on word sequence and the speed to examine the context of ambiguous words are not enough to make meaningful and complete translations solely by means of computers.

However, research in creating computer programs that understand stories has been more successful. After discarding the idea that a computer could achieve some understanding by having all the possible meanings of a word stored in its memory, researchers moved toward understanding coherent text.

Individual sentences in isolation can have many meanings. Roger Schank suggests that to illustrate the many meanings of a sentence, one think about the following: "We saw the Grand Canyon flying to Chicago." A computer could not understand such a sentence without some knowledge about airplanes and geography. Think how it might interpret such a sentence!

Or think about the sentence, "The policeman stopped the car with his hand." Your brain fills in the details of a person driving the car, putting on the brakes, and stopping when a policeman holds up his hand at an intersection.

Roger Schank and others who work in the field of natural-language understanding note that computer language must be able to draw inferences if it is to mirror human language. According to Schank, people have two kinds of knowledge about the world they live in: general and specific. General knowledge enables people to understand and interpret the actions of others because all human beings have similar needs and standard ways of getting them fulfilled. Specific knowledge applies to situations that have been experienced many times, such as watching a television program, ordering food in a restaurant, buying a ticket to a show or game, and brushing one's teeth. In each case, the sequence of events that takes place is predictable. He suggests that much of human behavior depends on the

Large space systems will require robots for fabrication, assembly, and construction in space. The robots could be guided by highly developed computers.

*—Jet Propulsion Laboratory*

learning of many scripts, or built-in knowledge of the world. The existence of common scripts makes it possible for people to draw inferences. These scripts can be considered as shorthand versions of everyday activities.

SAM (Script Applier Mechanism) is a system of computer programs that were written at the Yale University Artificial Intelligence Laboratory to make it possible to draw the inferences necessary to the understanding of stories. SAM processes stories in English, making some inferences as it does this. Restaurant stories are popular for showing SAM's ability to analyze the content and to answer questions.

An example of one of the simpler stories processed by SAM might be: "John went into a restaurant. He ordered a hamburger. He paid the check and left." SAM recognizes this as a restaurant story and draws inferences about things that are obvious to people. If SAM is questioned, "What did John eat?" the answer will be "John ate a hamburger," even though this is not actually specified in the story. SAM knows that John probably ate what he ordered.

SAM can answer questions by drawing inferences about much more complicated stories. On a factual level, SAM understands the story even though it has never eaten a hamburger. A person who has experienced eating a hamburger might understand the story on a different level, but even humans are said to understand stories about things they never experienced. In reading a story, SAM constructs a scenario that contains the events mentioned and also that could be reasonably inferred to have happened.

SAM is like a person trying to read stories in great detail. In other words, it does not skim. FRUMP (Fast Reading Understanding and Memory Program) is a program based on the idea of a script, but its scripts are not as detailed as SAM's. FRUMP can keep track of scripts it has used and how it has used them, so it can process stories faster than SAM, although it does so more superficially.

FRUMP can process a story that is six or seven lines long from a newspaper and summarize it in several languages. Each summary is a one-line sentence telling the most important points of the story.

PAM (Plan Applier Mechanism) is another program that was developed at Yale. It understands stories by recognizing the plans of the characters in the stories and their goals. PAM makes predictions about what kinds of events may occur. Consider the following story that is often used in explaining what PAM can do:

> John wanted some money. He got a gun and walked into a liquor store. He told the owner he wanted some money. The owner gave John the money and John left.

If you ask the computer what John did at the liquor store, it will respond that he robbed it to get some money. If you ask why the owner gave John the money, the computer will respond that the owner was afraid that John would hurt him.

Does the computer know more about the story than it has been told? Is this an intelligent computer? PAM programmer Professor Robert Wilensky, now at the University of California at Berkeley, will explain that the computer simply incorporates a sense of how people analyze and reason. It recognizes the presence of a threat because it was asked a question in the realm of its understanding. It was programmed to recognize a gun as a threatening weapon.

If you told the computer that John took his gun into the store and that he was given money for the gun, PAM would conclude that he was selling his gun. Getting money for the gun triggers the relationship of exchanging an object for money and PAM is programmed to know that this implies selling, for PAM is goal-oriented.

BORIS (a Better Organized Reading and Inference System) is the first attempt to combine the abilities demonstrated in SAM and PAM. This research project by Michael G. Dyer and Wendy G. Lehnert combines the inference techniques of scripts, plans, goals, and themes in a single program of reading stories and answering questions about them. It, too, is part of the Yale Artificial Intelligence Project.

A story that was chosen for BORIS follows, along with questions that were asked after the story was put into the computer and the answers that the computer gave.

### THE KIDNAP STORY
(Courtesy of Yale University Department of Computer Science)

John left his office early Friday afternoon so he could attend a going-away party for his friend Bill. Bill had been transferred to California. When he arrived there were lots of people and plenty of beer. Three years ago Bill had borrowed $50 from John, which John hoped to get back before Bill left. He was about to remind Bill about it when he was called to the phone. It was his wife, Mary, and she was hysterical. Mary had just received a call from a stranger who claimed to have kidnapped their daughter Susan. He said he would call again. John told Mary to stay at home, keep off the phone, and wait until he got there. John drove home immediately. Just as he walked in the door, the phone rang. John picked it up. But it was only Karen, one of Mary's friends. John told her Mary was out and hung up. Mary wanted to call the police but John thought they should wait. They were discussing this when Susan walked in the door. She had stayed after school for a gymnastics meet and taken a late bus home. Nothing had happened to her. It was all a hoax.

\* \* \* \* \* \* \* \* \* \* \* \* \* \* \* \* \* \* \* \* \* \*

Some representative BORIS questions and answers appear below. The questions are verbatim input to BORIS and the answers are verbatim computer output.

Q1: Why did John go to the party?
A1: He wanted to have a good time and he was Bill's friend
      and he wanted to get 50 dollars back from him.

Q2: Why did John leave the party?
A2: He was worried about Susan.

Q3: Why?
A3: Susan was kidnapped.

Q4: What happened to John at the party?
A4: He got a call from Mary.

Q5: Why did Mary call John at the party?
A5: She wanted to tell him about Susan's kidnapping.

Q6: Why did John want money from Bill?
A6: He borrowed 50 dollars from him.

Q7: Why didn't John talk to Bill?
A7: He was more worried about Susan.

Q8: Who called John at home?
A8: Karen.

Q9: Why?
A9: She wanted to talk to Mary.

Q10: Was Karen upset?
A10: No. She did not know about Susan's kidnapping.

Q11: Did John kidnap Susan?
A11: No. He was her father.

Q12: Where was Susan?
A12: She was attending a gymnastics meet.

Q13: What happened when Susan came home?
A13: John was relieved that she was safe.

Although the memory displayed by BORIS is indeed impressive, the researchers who developed this program point out that human memory is vastly superior to computer memory when dealing with episodes in the real world.

# 7.
# STAYING IN CONTROL

How bright should computers be allowed to become? No matter whether or not you consider computers to be thinking machines, you cannot deny that they are becoming increasingly capable. If a computer as intelligent as the human brain could be built, should it be built? This is a question that is being asked by laymen and experts alike.

Certainly today's computers are a long way from being as intelligent as a human being. Both the human brain and the computer brain depend on input and output. They both process information and they both use energy. The human brain is far more compact than any computer that holds amounts of data. Within about three pounds of living matter, the brain has the capacity to house between ten billion and a trillion or more bits of information. Every brain cell is directly connected to other brain cells with many connections, making possible a wealth of associations. The countless possible connections in the human brain makes it possible for a person to call on information from a rich store of past experiences. And the brain can handle thousands of tasks simultaneously.

An unmanned spacecraft guided by an onboard computer could navigate
between Jupiter and its satellites.

—Jet Propulsion Laboratory

Almost everyone agrees that computer ability is changing rapidly. Computers are said to have passed through four generations: from vacuum tubes to transistors to simple integrated circuits to VLSI (very large scale integration), which is the process of producing integrated circuits containing tens of thousands of electronic devices.

Today, there is much excitement about fifth generation computers, computers that can operate in more than "yes" or "no" terms. With artificial intelligence, the program tells the computer what to do without specifying exactly how to do it. In order to mimic human reasoning, special computer languages enable the computer to manipulate symbols rather than numbers. Decision-making rules and the knowledge used to reach a decision are separate. In other words, there is a shift from the data processing of conventional computers to an intelligent processing of knowledge.

When Japan announced in October 1981 its plans for a crash program to build fifth generation computers—those that could reason, make judgments, draw conclusions, and understand the written and spoken word—many experts pointed out that these have been goals of artificial intelligence researchers in England, the United States, and other countries for many years. The Japanese announcement created a challenge for many people who feel that the balance of power in the world will be affected by the large-scale development of such machines. In their book *The Fifth Generation,* Edward A. Feigenbaum and Pamela McCorduck call for a national plan of action in the United States, "a kind of space shuttle program for the knowledge systems of the future." Although some American observers have taken the Japanese announcement with skepticism, artificial intelligence has been widely acclaimed as the science of the future.

Traditional computers have long surpassed people at high-speed mathematics and logic, but people are far superior at "common sense" kinds of operations and creativity. Computers that learn by experience, ask questions and answer them, and create poetry and music are limited in their abilities. A computer that has the ability to decide what is relevant and what is not is very limited compared with the human brain.

As technology in artificial intelligence advances, more and more attention is being given to the question of what qualities intelligent machines should have. Some experts believe that qualities like selectivity should not even be granted to computers. Many believe that loneliness, fear, hate, love, and other emotions will always be beyond their scope.

While we are only in distant pursuit of intelligence that might simulate human intelligence in all its glory, a wide variety of people now are benefiting from the artificial intelligence research that has produced some programs exhibiting single aspects of it. Artificial intelligence is no longer considered to be a subject that is "blue sky," with little connection to the real world. Certainly, it has already accomplished part of its goal of making computers easier to use and more responsive to human needs. While trying to imitate the human brain, computer scientists may eventually learn things about the brain that we have not yet even thought of asking about.

One of the most practical and challenging of today's visions is in the development of telepersons, or surrogate workers for remote places, that have capabilities well beyond those of today's robots. The basic ideas for telepersons have already been worked out in a number of laboratories including M.I.T.,

James Albus, acting chief of the National Bureau of Standards Industrial Systems Division, with an experimental robot. The strobe light mounted just below the robot's "hands" illuminates objects in its field of vision with a narrow plane of light. A computer control deduces the rough shape and position of the objects from the image of this light plane as detected by the solid-state TV camera mounted above the wrist.

—*Beamie Young, National Bureau of Standards*

Stanford, Edinburgh, and Carnegie-Mellon universities. Professor Marvin Minsky of the M.I.T. Artificial Intelligence Laboratory describes a teleperson as one who could make dangerous jobs safe and comfortable. It could work in a nuclear reactor core, in the ocean's depths, or deep in a mine. When teleperson instruments are perfected, each motion of a person's arm, wrist, and fingers will be transmitted to its mechanical counterpart, and signals from the teleperson's sensors will be returned so that the human will know exactly what is happening in the distance. Professor Minsky estimates that it will be ten to 20 years before such a vision can become a reality. Even this timetable will require both aggressive work on the technology and funding of about one billion dollars. He believes, however, that the results could shape a new world of improved health, energy, and security.

Practical applications of artificial intelligence are becoming more numerous even in today's world in spite of the opponents who claimed that few, if any practical applications could come from research in this field. One of the most exciting developments is in the area of expert systems.

Expert systems are designed by having computer specialists together with the best expert or experts in a special field, such as organic chemistry, explore the reasoning the expert uses to apply his or her knowledge. The programmers codify the expert knowledge and mimic it in the computer program. When, say, a chemist explains that an answer to a problem was obtained just through a feeling of what was right or wrong, the artificial intelligence researcher helps the expert to become better aware of the kind of thinking used in the problem solving.

One of the first expert systems is DENDRAL, a system that used knowledge obtained from Joshua Lederberg, the

Anthony Barbera of the National Bureau of Standards Industrial Systems Division at the programming console of an NBS experimental robot. Instrumentation on the robot includes a vision system and sonic sensors used as proximity detectors.

*—Beamie Young, National Bureau of Standards*

famous geneticist. Developed at Stanford University in California, this system helps organic chemists determine the molecular structure of unknown compounds. In this and other expert systems, the computer learns to solve problems in the special area. After the computer has learned to solve problems by being a student of the experts, it can act as a teacher to human pupils.

Expert systems have been described as the closest thing to cloning a human mind, but their purpose is to make human beings more productive rather than replace them. MYCIN was an expert system that was written by medical doctor and computer scientist Edward Shortliffe. It was able to diagnose infectious diseases quite well, but it lacked the awareness of its limitations. Professor Randall Davis of Massachusetts Institute of Technology suggested that if it were confronted with a bicycle that had a flat tire, it would do its best to find the proper antibiotic for the bicycle. Expert systems have been compared with idiot savants, people who are brilliant in one area but not much good at anything else.

Some expert systems such as MYCIN have been used as a basis for many other programs by emptying them of their knowledge. In the case of MYCIN, its knowledge of bacteria is removed. EMYCIN, the shell of the original program, has been applied to many different tasks, such as freeing stuck oil-drilling bits, diagnosing lung disease, and pinpointing the cause of computer failures. A number of companies sell programming shells that can be used to help a company design its own expert system.

Today's expert systems are thought of as knowledgeable assistants or consultants, and they are used in many fields. For example, when alarms go off in a nuclear power plant, this kind of system makes the knowledge of many experts available for consultation at any hour of the night or day. ONCOCIN is a system that helps cancer specialists plan drug therapy for their patients. Another expert system can help the Navy track fires on aircraft carriers and another may help weathermen to predict floods. At Campbell Soup, an expert system can ask maintenance workers a series of technical questions about the state of the valves, cooling sprays, and other equipment. Based on this, it can provide information about which valve to change in order to eliminate a problem such as an incorrect cooking temperature. At Northwest Orient, an expert system can evaluate how many discount and how many full-price seats should be offered on each flight to make the most money for the company.

A small number of businesses that design expert systems have emerged, supported chiefly by large companies that hope to profit financially from the new software. Some companies sell programming shells which other companies can use to design their expert systems. Many expert programs are still very expensive, but this kind of "smart software" is expected to become far more common as prices decline.

One of the most exciting expert systems is BACON, which was developed by Patrick Langley at Carnegie-Mellon University. It was named for Frances Bacon, a philosopher of the Elizabethan period who was an early proponent of inductive reasoning and the experimental method. When the program BACON is supplied with data from famous scientific experiments, it can rediscover the laws that the scientists discovered many years ago, such as Ohm's law, Kepler's third law of planetary motion, and Boyle's law of gases. The program has not discovered any new scientific laws, but some scientists believe that BACON or similar programs may be able to do so.

Human beings learn from their mistakes, but in the case of expert systems, reprogramming is needed. In many cases, computers do worst what people do best. For example, pattern recognition is difficult for computers but easy for people. You can recognize a person by looking at him full face or at almost any angle, something computers cannot do.

Professor Donald Michie of the Machine Intelligence Unit at the University of Edinburgh believes that expert systems may be the answer to the problem of letting people question a computer on why it reached a decision. Traditionally, computers are "number crunchers" or "information sifters." For example, most computer chess programs rely on what is called brute force, a method in which they just churn quickly through all possible moves and use their high-speed processing ability to weigh options rather than using the trial-and-error type of reasoning that humans use to make decisions.

Since expert systems reach conclusions through a process of reasoning that is like human reasoning (one that is based on logic and experience) they may provide a "human window." In these systems, people can understand the reasoning behind computer results. Professor Michie warns that such a window is needed to provide humans with a way of staying in command. In other words, this is the kind of artificial intelligence that will provide a way to monitor and control machine behavior. When computers arrive at conclusions through brute force, they do so with a speed and complexity that is beyond human comprehension.

Professor Michie gives an example of the bad consequences that can result when there is no "human window": there was much confusion and delay during Three Mile Island's nuclear mishap when people could not quickly understand the meaning of computer-controlled alarm systems.

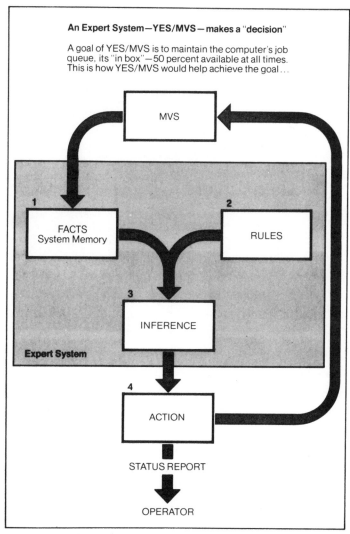

**An Expert System—YES/MVS—makes a "decision"**

A goal of YES/MVS is to maintain the computer's job queue, its "in box"—50 percent available at all times. This is how YES/MVS would help achieve the goal...

MVS

**1** FACTS System Memory

**2** RULES

**3** INFERENCE

Expert System

**4** ACTION

STATUS REPORT

OPERATOR

YES/MVS. This diagram illustrates how the experimental system YES/MVS makes a "decision." The goal of YES/MVS in this example is to keep 50 percent of the computer's job queue available at all times. The expert system will combine the facts it has about the system's condition with the rules it possesses, to make an inference. It will either use the inference about the system to get more data, or to make a "decision" about what to do in order to achieve or maintain the goal.

For example:
1 MVS says queue space is low (FACT)
2 ... and a RULE says that when space is low, query the printer's state ...
3 ... which is an INFERENCE ...
4 ... which results in a query (ACTION) to MVS ...
... which starts the process over again, by determining that ...
1 (FACT) a. The printer has a few short jobs
      b. The printer is holding a long job
      c. The printer is limited to printing 30,000 lines
... combining these FACTS with the
2 ... RULE that if a, b, and c are true, the correct
3 ... INFERENCE is to raise the printer's line limit ...
4 ... an ACTION is initiated: raise the printer's line limit.

The action frees the computer's job queue, which was reacting to the large printing job on hold. This achieves the goal, i.e., the system's job queue becomes at least 50 percent available.

—Courtesy of IBM

Many artificial intelligence researchers stress the importance of remaining in control by making certain that programs can examine their own behavior and tell humans how they reach their conclusions. They point out that machines must not be given authority without responsibility.

Some scientists believe that there is less danger in the possibility of machines taking over than there is in humans becoming dependent on machines.

Very few people realize how much artificial intelligence research is being carried out by the Defense Department of the United States. The armed forces are involved in programs that range from smarter tanks to the computer systems that could become the core of the Star Wars defense system.

In Machine Intelligence Technology, which combines advances in artificial intelligence, computer science, and micro-electronics, the Army is trying to develop a new breed of robots that can be used in connection with cruise missiles, underwater robots, and tanks. Someday, intelligent robots may do sentry duty, perform mine disposal, and explore hostile and inaccessible terrain. Land vehicle systems could support such activities as ammunition handling and weapons delivery, and missions involving deep penetration of reconnaissance aircraft.

A new breed of walking machines appears promising for work in many industries as well as for military uses. Imagine a robot with six legs walking around a warehouse, checking out a trouble spot in a nuclear power plant, or working on assembly lines. A "mother and ducklings" scenario is being considered by the Army in which a squadron of robot tanks would be led across a battlefield by one manned tank. The robots would take their cues from the leader, but once they were involved in battle, they could operate on their own.

The Terregator, an example of experiments in Machine Intelligence Technology, is a vehicle with six wheels and television cameras that needs no driver. Different versions of this experimental vehicle are being developed according to the type of equipment to be carried. They are powered by either gasoline or electricity.

Professor William Whittaker, a principal scientist of the Terregator project at Carnegie-Mellon's Robotic Institute, has told about the time the Terregator embarrassed its creators when they took it for a spin in a neighboring park. The vehicle was aimed down a wooded path and it was navigating the curves nicely until they became sharper. Then it veered off the path, climbed a tree to the height of four feet, and clawed at the bark of the tree. Scientists figured that the Terregator's model of a road fit the tree more than the path, and went to work to remedy this.

Research and development projects similar to those at Carnegie-Mellon University are under way at a number of artificial intelligence laboratories. Scientists hope to see vehicles moving independently at reasonable speed in constrained environments in the near future, but they disagree about the time frame for those moving in the real world where other moving objects and varied terrain are present.

Scientists also disagree about how much computers can be expected to act as problem solvers. Although there will be problems they can never solve, some experts claim that there are systems that already surpass human intelligence; others claim that they never will. Some look ahead to a new relationship between computers and people in which they are completely dependent on each other for survival. Others point out computer limitations—things they never will be able to do.

Even the definition of artificial intelligence is a subject of controversy. Several scientists have noted that the definition changes as research moves forward. For example, computer vision, once regarded as a part of artificial intelligence research, now is seen by many people as part of general computer development. Larry Tessler is credited as being the first to suggest that artificial intelligence is "whatever hasn't been done yet." Perhaps this is because of the fact that once a mental function is programmed, people tend to stop considering it as an essential ingredient of thinking. But for those who are willing to accept a limited definition of the word "intelligence," artificial intelligence has arrived.

Today's computers are a hundred times faster than the supercomputers of ten years ago, but even these will seem feeble before many years have passed. Artificial intelligence experts foresee even more exciting applications of computers that think when computer power is increased. Research to increase computer power is proceeding on many fronts. For example, instead of etching silicon chips with visible light, X-rays may be used to replace the visible light. Another alternative is laying down the circuits molecule by molecule.

Microchips made of gallium arsenide instead of silicon are already going into mass production. Although these chips are more expensive, they do the job faster and more efficiently than silicon chips. Answers to the search for greater capacity may come from still other approaches. For example, some of tomorrow's computers may use beams of modulated laser light rather than electric current.

Interfacing computers with living parts is a subject of controversy, but one that intrigues many experts who are trying to increase the ability of computers to learn and recognize

In the future, a small tethered robot may bring surface samples to a large automatic processing station on Mars. All robot and processing procedures may be controlled by a fifth generation computer.

*—Jet Propulsion Laboratory*

complex patterns. However, if bacterial inputs were used for computers, the bacteria would determine the program rather than the human programmer. Could this lead to humans no longer being in control?

Will the computer become a Joseph Golem? Are there things machines should not be allowed to do? Will humans remain in control?

If scientists proceed with caution and healthy fear, there is more reason to believe that intelligent machines will become powerful allies than that they will become man's enemies. In any case, the search for artificial intelligence goes on.

# SUGGESTED READING

Albus, James. *Brains, Behavior and Robotics*. Peterborough, N.H.: BYTE Books, 1981.

Aleksander, Igor, and Piers Burnett. *Reinventing Man*. New York: Holt, Rinehart and Winston, 1983.

Ardley, Neil. *Computers*. New York: Warwick, 1983.

Asimov, Isaac. *Robots: Machines in Man's Image*. Avenel, N.J.: Crown Publishers, 1985.

Changeux, Jean-Pierre. *Neuronal Man: The Biology of the Mind*. New York: Pantheon Books, 1985.

Evans, Christopher. *The Micro Millennium*. New York: Viking Press, 1979.

Feigenbaum, Edward A., and Pamela McCorduck. *The Fifth Generation*. Reading, Mass.: Addison-Wesley, 1983, and New York.: New American Library, 1984.

Griffin, Donald R. *Animal Thinking.* Cambridge: Harvard University Press, 1984.

Harmon, Paul, and David King. *Expert Systems: Artificial Intelligence in Business.* New York: Wiley, 1985.

Kent, Ernest. *The Brain of Men and Machines.* New York: McGraw-Hill, 1981.

Levy, Steven. *Hackers: Heroes of the Computer Revolution.* New York: Doubleday, 1984.

Logsdon, Tom. *The Robot Revolution.* New York: Simon and Schuster, 1984.

McCorduck, Pamela. *Machines Who Think: A Personal Inquiry into the History and Prospects of Artificial Intelligence.* San Francisco: W.H. Freeman, 1979.

Michie, Donald, and Rorey Johnston. *The Creative Computer: Machine Intelligence and Human Knowledge.* New York: Viking Press, 1984.

Minsky, Marvin, ed. *Robotics: The First Authoritative Report from the Ultimate High-Tech Frontier.* Garden City, N.Y.: Anchor/Doubleday, 1985.

Reid, T.R. *The Chip: How Two Americans Invented the Microchip and Launched a Revolution.* New York: Simon and Schuster, 1985.

Rose, Frank. *Into the Heart of the Mind: An American Quest for Artificial Intelligence.* New York: Harper and Row, 1984.

Schank, Roger C., with Peter G. Childes. *The Cognitive Computer: On Language, Learning and Artificial Intelligence.* Reading, Mass.: Addison-Wesley, 1984.

Simon, Geoff. *Are Computers Alive? Evolution and New Life Forms.* Cambridge: Birkhauser Books, 1983.

Turkle, Sherry. *The Second Self: Computers and the Human Spirit.* New York: Simon and Schuster, 1984.

Winston, Patrick H., and Karen A. Prendergast. *The AI Business: The Commercial Use of Artificial Intelligence.* Cambridge: MIT Press, 1984.

# INDEX